RELIGIONS
OF THE WORLD

written by Jason Elliot *and* Dene Schofield
illustrated by L R Galante

CONTENTS

WHAT IS RELIGION?

People have always tried to understand the mysteries of the natural forces that affect their lives. Religions have helped many people understand these areas of life. In doing so, religions have shaped the world and the way people live.

Religious symbols

1 The Golden Temple (Sikhism)
2 Crucifix (Christianity)
3 The Koran (Islam)

4 Diwali celebration (Hinduism)
5 Praying monk (Buddhism)
6 Seder (Judaism)

FAITH AND WORSHIP

Religious **faith** consists of a belief in a god or many gods, or sometimes a great spirit or invisible power that influences a person's life. Most religions have special places where people go to pray, or a **sacred** natural site. The stories and guiding rules of most religions are contained in writings that are considered sacred.

Gods

Many religions are based on the existence of a single god. Others have several different gods. In the Hindu religion, for example, god has many forms. One of these is Vishnu, who is worshipped as a human, but also as an animal such as a bird or a fish.

Religious leaders

There are often guides to help people understand their religion. The Pope is the leader of the Roman Catholic Church, and gives help and guidance to millions of Catholic Christians.

Festivals

Religions often have festivals to remember events or to **worship** special gods. The Hindu festival of light, **Diwali**, is celebrated with decorations and special foods.

Afterlife

Most religions have ideas on what happens to people after death. In Chinese faith people worship their ancestors with offerings of food and lighted incense sticks.

Prayer

In many religions, prayer is an important part of worship. Jewish people pray and light candles when they celebrate **Hanukkah**.

Rules

All religions have guiding rules to help people understand their god or gods, and to learn how to treat others, how to live together and how to meet the challenges of life.

ANCIENT RELIGIONS

Early people believed in gods of nature, and worshipped the planets and stars. There is a lot of **archaeological** evidence of this. Stonehenge, in England, for example, is thought to be an early religious site. It was built around 5,000 years ago, and is made up of gigantic stones, arranged in a circle.

Hunter-gatherers

Hunter-gatherers painted images of animals on their cave walls. This may have been done as an act of worship to their gods of nature, and to bring them luck in hunting.

Sumerians

The Sumerians were farmers and inventors who lived about 5,000 years ago in the Middle East. They built huge temples called ziggurats to honour their gods. The remains of a ziggurat can be seen today at Ur, in Iraq.

Egyptians

The ancient Egyptians worshipped many gods and built beautiful temples and pyramids. These were huge tombs where important people were **mummified** and buried with all their valuable belongings.

Greeks

The ancient Greeks had legends about gods and goddesses, and heroes, who were part god and part human. They built temples such as the Parthenon in Athens.

Romans

The early Romans believed in many of the Greek gods and also in lesser gods called **numina** who looked after all aspects of life. Later, Christianity was adopted as the official Roman religion and the worship of other gods was forbidden.

American Indians

The Indians of North America believed in the spirits of the natural world, such as mountains and rivers, and also in the spirits of animals. Some American Indians carved images of their spirit gods on totem poles. These were tall wooden poles that often represented families and the myths and legends of American Indian people.

9

DEVELOPMENT OF RELIGIONS

The main religions of the world today have developed over a long period of time and have gone through many changes. Many early religions have disappeared completely. Religions have also been affected by each other. The ancient religion of Zoroastrianism has influenced Judaism, Christianity and Islam, all of which

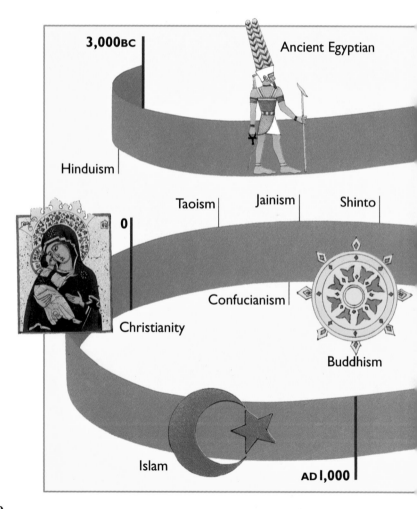

3,000BC

Ancient Egyptian

Hinduism

Taoism   Jainism   Shinto

0

Confucianism

Christianity

Buddhism

Islam

AD1,000

arose in the countries of the Middle East and share many of the same traditions. Other religions such as Buddhism and Shinto arose in the Far East, and also have many similarities. Some later religions grew from a specific religion and later became separate, such as Sikhism, which evolved from the Hindu religion.

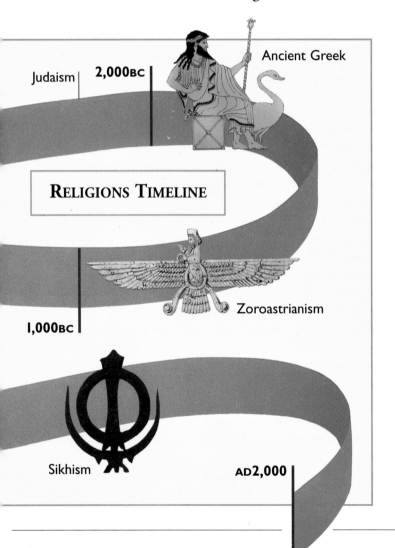

Judaism | **2,000BC**

Ancient Greek

RELIGIONS TIMELINE

Zoroastrianism

1,000BC

Sikhism

AD2,000

JUDAISM

The birth of Judaism came about nearly 4,000 years ago, when Abraham and the Jewish people made a promise to worship only one god, called Yahweh. Later, Moses became a great leader of the Jews and helped them to establish their religion in freedom outside Egypt, where they had lived in slavery. This was called the Exodus, and is remembered with deep feeling by all Jews.

JEWISH SYMBOL
The Star of David is the symbol of the Jewish religion.

Synagogue
A synagogue is a Jewish place of worship. On Saturday, the day of the **Sabbath**, Jews offer prayers and sing psalms from the Old Testament of the Bible.

The Torah
The Torah is a collection of traditions and teachings including articles on history, worship, and instructions about the Jewish way of life. In every synagogue, the Torah is written on scrolls in Hebrew, the ancient Jewish language.

The Wailing Wall

After the **persecution** of the Jews during the Second World War, Jews from all over the world came to live in Israel, their religious homeland. The Wailing Wall is part of an ancient Jewish temple in Jerusalem, where Jews come to pray and remember the history of their people.

Rabbis

A rabbi is a Jewish teacher who gives religious instruction, performs services and guides the community. On the Jewish New Year, the rabbi blows a ram's horn to remind people to listen to God.

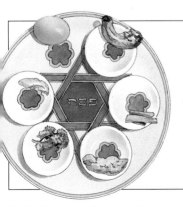

PASSOVER

*Passover is an important Jewish festival which **commemorates** the Jewish people's release from slavery in Egypt. Special foods are eaten, such as unleavened bread and salt water. The meal is called the Seder and is eaten from a special plate.*

CHRISTIANITY

Christianity takes its name from Jesus Christ, who was born nearly 2,000 years ago in the Jewish town of Bethlehem. At the age of about 30 he began to teach new ideas about God, which became the foundation of Christian belief. Christ had many followers, but his teachings upset the non-Christian Romans, who were the religious authorities of the time, and they **crucified** him.

CHRISTIAN SYMBOL
A cross is the most popular symbol of Christianity, representing the way Jesus died.

Disciples
Jesus gave special training to twelve men, called the Disciples. After his death they wrote down his teachings and helped to spread his ideas to different parts of the world, and Christian communities began to grow.

The Crusades
In Medieval times, a series of wars, called the Crusades, were fought between Muslims and knights from western Europe. They both wanted to control the city of Jerusalem.

The Bible

The most important book to Christians is the Bible. Its New Testament contains stories of the life of Jesus and his teachings. In the early years of Christianity, monks copied out the Bible in beautiful handwriting and decorated it with colourful pictures.

Baptism

Baptism is a ceremony which marks a person's admission into the Christian faith and washes away their sins. Babies are baptised when a priest or minister puts **holy** water onto the baby's head, but in some churches, adults are baptised by being plunged into holy water.

Communion

One of the most important Christian ceremonies is Holy Communion. A priest or minister gives people bread and wine, just as Jesus is said to have done at the 'Last Supper' with his Disciples. This was the last occasion Jesus was with his Disciples before he was crucified.

BRANCHES OF CHRISTIANITY

As time passed, people developed different ways of understanding Jesus and his teachings. In 1504 the Church divided into two **sects**. The Catholic Church was established in Rome and the Orthodox Church in Constantinople, now called Istanbul, in Turkey. Later in the 16th century, the Protestant Church broke away from the Catholic Church.

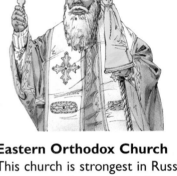

Protestant Church
The Protestant Church was founded by Martin Luther, a German monk. He wanted the Bible to be translated from Latin into other languages so that more people could read it.

Eastern Orthodox Church
This church is strongest in Russia and Eastern Europe. Its followers believe it has kept more of the original Christian traditions. Its customs are different from the Catholic and Protestant sects.

QUAKERS
The Society of Friends is a Christian group founded in the 17th century. Early believers used to tremble with religious emotion, so were given the name Quakers. They have no leader and individuals speak when they want to.

Icons

Icons are painted images of Jesus or Christian saints important to the Eastern Orthodox Church. People pray and light candles in front of their favourite icons.

Monastic tradition

Many early Christians founded monasteries or communities where people could devote their lives to prayer and work according to their idea of God.

Christian unity

All different Christian groups believe in God and the example of Jesus, although they may interpret his teaching differently.

Today, the leaders of different groups try to work together for the benefit of all Christians, to help people all over the world.

A CATHEDRAL

A cathedral is an important Christian church built in the shape of a cross to commemorate Jesus. In medieval times, when most cathedrals were built, people made **pilgrimages** from great distances to come and visit cathedrals, which were the largest and most beautiful buildings in the country.

Altar

Bishop
Any church that has a bishop is called a cathedral. A bishop is a very senior kind of priest who has authority to perform important services.

Altar
The altar is used for the service of Holy Communion. It is traditionally at the eastern end of the cathedral, and is separated from the other areas by a communion rail.

Building
The largest cathedrals took so many years to build that craftsmen might have spent their whole lives working on just one part.

Dome

Zulla
(prayer hall)

Mosque
Muslims pray in a building called
a mosque. Each one has one or
more towers – minarets – where
a man known as the Muezzin
calls people to prayer. The
inside of the mosque is
decorated with patterns of
mosaic tiles and Arabic writing,
but there are no statues or
paintings. The floor is covered
with large carpets and there
are no chairs.

Minbar
(reading desk)

Tower

Transept

Buttress

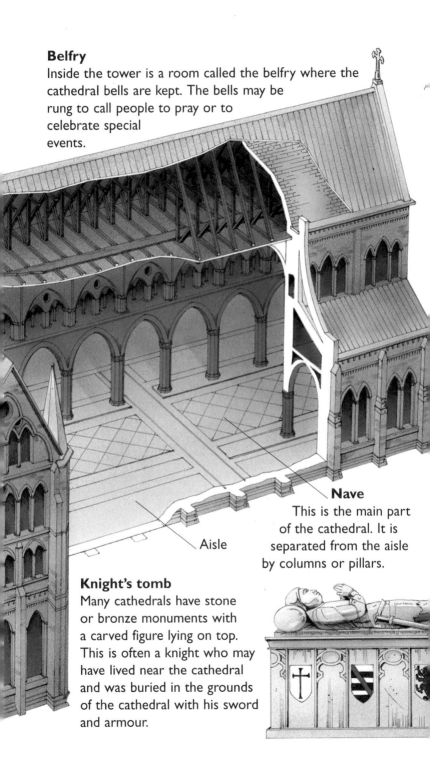

Belfry
Inside the tower is a room called the belfry where the cathedral bells are kept. The bells may be rung to call people to pray or to celebrate special events.

Nave
This is the main part of the cathedral. It is separated from the aisle by columns or pillars.

Aisle

Knight's tomb
Many cathedrals have stone or bronze monuments with a carved figure lying on top. This is often a knight who may have lived near the cathedral and was buried in the grounds of the cathedral with his sword and armour.

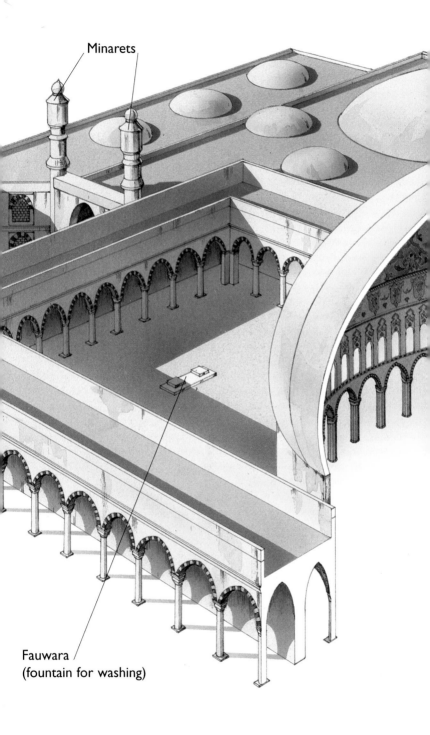

Minarets

Fauwara
(fountain for washing)

The interiors of cathedrals are decorated with tall arches and columns, statues, mosaics and stained glass windows. These windows are made up of many small pieces of coloured glass, put together to show a picture. The picture usually represents a story from the Bible.

Pulpit
The pulpit is a raised platform inside the cathedral. It is the place from which the bishop speaks or reads to the congregation during services.

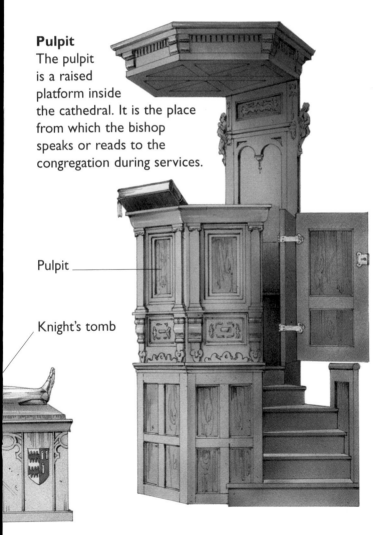

Pulpit

Knight's tomb

ISLAM

Islam is the religion of Muslims who follow the teaching of the prophet Mohammed. He was born in the city of Mecca, Saudi Arabia around AD 570. Mohammed is said to have received messages from God and his messenger, the angel Gabriel. Mohammed claimed that Islam was a continuation of the Jewish and Christian religions, and that he was the world's last prophet. Islam spread over a vast area of the world within a few centuries.

ISLAMIC SYMBOL
This symbol of Islam, is seen on the flags of many Islamic countries.

Prayer

Prayer is a very important part of the Muslim way of life. Muslims pray five times a day, either in private or with others. They recite verses of the Koran during prayers and touch their foreheads to the ground. Wherever they may be, Muslims kneel in the direction of the holy city of Mecca when praying.

Koran

The Koran is the most sacred book to Muslims. It contains many of the same stories as the Bible, as well as guidance on all aspects of life. Many Muslims learn the entire Koran by heart.

Mihrab

In the mosque, the mihrab shows the direction of the city of Mecca. The mihrab is often decorated with many different patterns, coloured tiles, and has verses from the Koran carved round it.

The Ka'bah

The Ka'bah is a temple inside the Great Mosque at Mecca. It is the most sacred site of the Islamic world. Many Muslims make pilgrimages to see it. Inside the Ka'bah is a sacred black stone.

HINDUISM

Hinduism is an ancient religion which originated more than 4,000 years ago in India. There are thousands of different Hindu gods, but all Hindus believe in Brahman, the great universal force behind life. Hindus take a personal approach to worship – they find their own way to understanding God. Hindu teaching is contained in books called the Upanishads and Vedas.

HINDU SYMBOL
*This symbol is made up of three letters which form a Hindu **mantra**.*

Brahma

Shiva

Gods

As Hinduism is such an ancient religion, it has absorbed many different traditions. Some say there are millions of Hindu gods! Three of the most important gods are Brahma, Shiva and Vishnu.

Vishnu

WORSHIP
*Hindus go to temples to worship, but most homes also have a shrine with a statue or picture of one or more gods. Hindus offer prayers, as well as fruit or flowers, and burn incense at shrines. This ceremony is called a **puja**.*

Sacred cow

Many Hindus believe that when people die, their souls are reborn in animal or human form. The way a soul is reborn is caused by a person's actions, or **karma**, in this life. Animals are respected and many Hindus are vegetarian. The cow is an especially sacred animal and is never eaten.

Holy river

The Ganges river, in India, has a deep symbolic meaning for Hindus. Thousands of people wash in the river every day. After death, many Hindus are **cremated** and have their ashes scattered on the river, in the belief that their souls will be carried on to the next life.

Gandhi

Mohandas Gandhi was an Indian Hindu who campaigned for the rights of Indian people in South Africa, and for Indian independence from Britain. His belief in Hinduism led him to show people how they could protest without violence. The Indian people gave him the name Mahatma, which means a great man.

BUDDHISM

Buddhism began when a rich, young Indian prince called Siddhartha Gautama thought about how much suffering there was in the world. He gave up his privileged lifestyle and spent many years searching for a solution to life's problems. Many of them were caused by people's desire for things and beliefs. Gautama founded a religion which had no gods and became the Buddha. His guide to Buddhism is known as the Four Noble Truths.

BUDDHIST SYMBOL
One of the symbols of Buddhism is a lotus flower.

The Four Noble Truths

1 Life is full of suffering.
2 Suffering is caused by desire.
3 Stopping desire ends suffering.
4 Desire can be ended by following the noble path –

a path to peace consisting of: right beliefs, right intentions, right speech, right behaviour, right concentration, right effort, right thinking and right work.

Holy place

In India, a burial mound containing the relics of Buddha is a holy place for Buddhists.

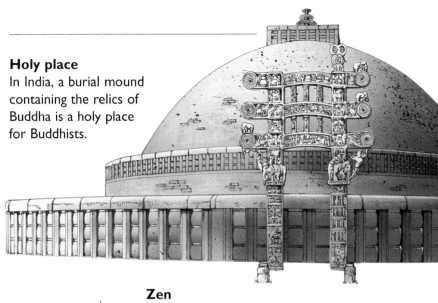

Zen

Buddhism has spread to many parts of the world, especially the Far East. **Zen** Buddhism a popular branch of Buddhism has many followers in Europe and America.

Pagoda

Pagodas are towers with many floors, often seen in southeast Asia. They have beautifully carved roofs and beams. Pagodas are often used as Buddhist temples and have images of Buddha inside.

Buddhist monks

In Thailand, many boys become monks at some time in their lives. They give up their belongings, study the Buddha's teachings, and meditate each day to calm the emotions and clear the mind.

RELIGIONS IN THE FAR EAST

In China, about 2,500 years ago, a wise man called Confucius founded a way of life known as Confucianism. He taught people the importance of order, goodness and courtesy as well as respect for parents and ancestors. Another Chinese teacher, Lao Tzu, showed people a way of living in harmony with the natural order of the universe, which he called the Tao.

The Kitchen and Door God
Far Eastern religions worship many gods. In most homes there is a portrait of the Kitchen God, as well as the Door God on either side of the front door to keep away evil spirits.

Confucius
Confucius believed in caring for the family and society. He encouraged the learning of poetry, music and history and his example is well respected in Chinese tradition.

Scholars
Learning is a major part of many religions. Scholars often write the ideas of a religion in beautiful books and scripts.

Taoism

This Taoist symbol represents yin and yang – the opposing forces in the universe, such as winter and summer, male and female.

Dragon dance

During festivals such as the Chinese New Year, celebrations include a dragon dance with acrobats inside a brightly coloured dragon costume. There is music and drumming and lots of fireworks are lit in the streets.

SHINTO

Shinto is an ancient Japanese religion and is still followed, in some form.

There are many Shinto gods, called Kami, which are worshipped at shrines.

Many Shinto traditions still exist today such as the wearing of beautiful robes, called kimonos.

OLD AND NEW RELIGIONS

There are many faiths in the world today. Some have grown out of older religious traditions, but have taken into account changes in the world. The Baha'i faith, for example, was founded in the 1860s in Persia (now Iran). It is based on Islam and has become accepted as a religion in its own right.

SIKH SYMBOL
This symbol of the Sikh religion represents two swords, to defend the faith at all times.

Sikhism
The Sikh religion was founded in India by Guru Nanak 500 years ago. Sikhs believe in a single God and follow a text called the Granth. Temples used for worship also provide food and shelter for the needy. The most holy site for Sikhs is the Golden Temple in Amritsar, India.

Granth
Sikhs read passages from the Granth during worship in their temples.

Jainism

Jainism originated in India about 2,500 years ago. Jains do not worship a god, but believe in the soul of humans and animals. Living creatures must not be harmed, so Jains do not eat meat or fish, and often wear a mask so that insects are not accidentally swallowed. Like Hindus, Jains have a strong belief in karma – that every action during life has an effect.

Rastafarianism

Rastafarianism is named after Ras Tafari, the Ethiopian emperor (in East Africa) of the 1930s. Rastafarians believe that God will help their people return to Africa. They study the Bible, especially the Old Testament. They wear their hair in special braids called dreadlocks, and cover their heads with a large hat.

Aboriginal religion

The Aboriginal people have always lived in Australia. Like the Indians of North America they have many sacred natural sites, and different names for the spirits of the land. They paint images of these spirits on rocks and caves. Special ceremonies are performed when someone is born or dies.

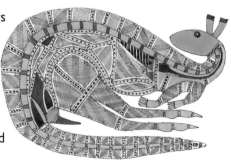

RELIGION FOR EVERYONE

Today we live in a world in which people follow different religions. Unfortunately, some people are still persecuted for their religious beliefs. Respect and kindness towards other people are important teachings in all religions, and religious freedom and tolerance are important because they allow people to follow their own beliefs.

The main religions in the world today

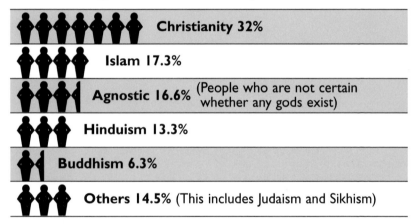

Christianity 32%

Islam 17.3%

Agnostic 16.6% (People who are not certain whether any gods exist)

Hinduism 13.3%

Buddhism 6.3%

Others 14.5% (This includes Judaism and Sikhism)

CHRISTIAN CHURCH IN INDIA
Indian society is made up mainly of Hindus. However, in Simla, a city in northern India, there is a Christian church, which is attended by many Christian Indians. This shows that different religions can exist peacefully together.

Religious differences
Throughout history, much suffering and many wars have been caused by religious differences between people. It is becoming clearer that discussion and cooperation are more important, especially in the face of urgent world problems such as damage to our environment or poverty. The World Congress of Faiths is trying to build better relations between people of different beliefs.

Dove of peace
The dove is an ancient symbol of peace and hope. Many people believe that the day will come when there is no longer any religious conflict or persecution in the world.

Mother Theresa
Religious leaders understand the need to help others, whatever their race or religion. Mother Theresa is a Christian nun who lives in Calcutta, India. For years she has worked in many countries to help poor or sick people. She is an example to the world that love for others can bridge the differences between all religions.

AMAZING RELIGIONS FACTS

- **Pilgrims' progress** Every year over three million Muslims make a pilgrimage, or hajj, to the holy city of Mecca, in Saudi Arabia.

- **Reading and writing** The Christian Bible has been translated into more than 1,000 languages and is the most widely read book in the world.

- **The sacred book** In Sikhism the word Guru means the bearer of God's words. The founder of Sikhism, Guru Nanak was followed by nine more Gurus, all of whom developed Sikhism as a religion. The last of these Gurus declared that the Sikh's holy book, the Granth, should be the final Guru, and it is still seen as this today.

- **Towering tomb** Of all the pyramids built by the ancient Egyptians, the Great Pyramid of Cheops is the largest in the world. It is 147 metres high and covers an area of over 50,000 square metres.

- **Slow progress** The famous cathedral at Canterbury, England, has undergone a lot of rebuilding since it was started in 1067 by the Normans. In 1174, the section that housed the choir burned down, and was not fully restored until 1220. Then in 1377 the nave was knocked down and rebuilt by 1405. Finally, one of the towers was rebuilt in 1498, over 400 years since work first began.

- **Poetry in motion** One of the most important texts in Hinduism is the Mahabharata. This poem contains 200,000 verses and is the longest poem in the world.

GLOSSARY

Archaeology The study of past human life and activities, using fossils, relics, buildings or artefacts.

Commemorate To remember a special occasion by a ceremony or event.

Cremate To burn a dead body and reduce it to ashes before burial.

Crucify To execute a person by nailing or binding their hands and feet to a cross and leaving them to die.

Diwali The Hindu festival of light which is celebrated with decorations and special foods.

Faith A belief in the traditional principles of a religion.

Hanukkah An eight-day Jewish holiday in December.

Holy Something connected with a god, or gods, which is very important to a religion.

Karma The actions and behaviour of people during their lives that decides their fate after death.

Mantra A word or sound used as a religious chant.

Mummify To prepare a body for burial by treating it with preservatives and then wrapping it in linen bandages.

Numina Any one of the ancient Romans' lesser gods.

Persecute To cause suffering to a person or people because of their beliefs.

Pilgrimage A journey to a shrine or sacred place for religious purposes.

Puja The Hindu ceremony where incense is burnt at shrines, and prayers, fruit and flowers are offered to gods.

Sabbath In the Jewish religion, this is Saturday. Jews see it as a day of rest.

Sacred Something that is to be respected and is very holy.

Sect A group that breaks away from an established religion.

Worship The way people honour their god or gods. This may be with prayers, songs, offerings or thoughts.

Zen A Japanese sect of Buddhism which promotes religious meditation.

INDEX *(Entries in **bold** refer to an illustration)*